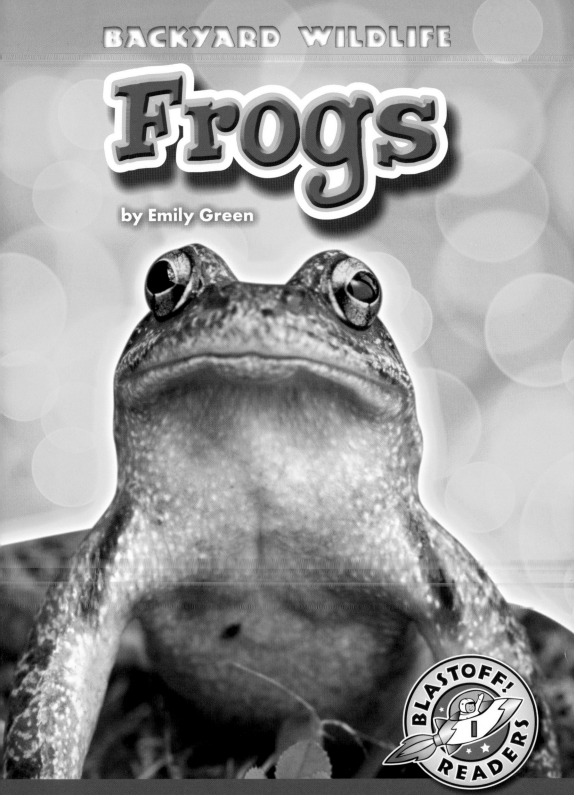

BACKYARD WILDLIFE

Frogs

by Emily Green

BELLWETHER MEDIA · MINNEAPOLIS, MN

Note to Librarians, Teachers, and Parents:

Blastoff! Readers are carefully developed by literacy experts and combine standards-based content with developmentally appropriate text.

Level 1 provides the most support through repetition of high-frequency words, light text, predictable sentence patterns, and strong visual support.

Level 2 offers early readers a bit more challenge through varied simple sentences, increased text load, and less repetition of high-frequency words.

Level 3 advances early-fluent readers toward fluency through increased text and concept load, less reliance on visuals, longer sentences, and more literary language.

Level 4 builds reading stamina by providing more text per page, increased use of punctuation, greater variation in sentence patterns, and increasingly challenging vocabulary.

Level 5 encourages children to move from "learning to read" to "reading to learn" by providing even more text, varied writing styles, and less familiar topics.

Whichever book is right for your reader, Blastoff! Readers are the perfect books to build confidence and encourage a love of reading that will last a lifetime!

This edition first published in 2011 by Bellwether Media, Inc.

No part of this publication may be reproduced in whole or in part without written permission of the publisher. For information regarding permission, write to Bellwether Media, Inc., Attention: Permissions Department, 5357 Penn Avenue South, Minneapolis, MN 55419.

Library of Congress Cataloging-in-Publication Data
Green, Emily K., 1966–
Frogs / by Emily Green.
    p. cm. — (Blastoff! readers: Backyard wildlife)
Includes bibliographical references and index.
Summary: "Developed by literacy experts for students in kindergarten through grade three, this book introduces frogs to young readers through leveled text and related photos"—Provided by publisher.
ISBN 978-1-60014-442-4 (hardcover : alk. paper)
1. Frogs—Juvenile literature. I. Title.
QL668.E2G68 2010
597.8'9–dc22   2010006433

Text copyright © 2011 by Bellwether Media, Inc. BLASTOFF! READERS and associated logos are trademarks and/or registered trademarks of Bellwether Media, Inc.

Printed in the United States of America, North Mankato, MN.

080110   1162

Contents

Frogs are animals with strong back legs. Their legs help them jump.

Most frogs are green, brown, or gray. Many frogs have spots or stripes.

Frogs use the color
of their skin to hide.
They blend in with
leaves, grass,
or branches.

Most frogs start out as **tadpoles**. They have tails like fish. They swim in water.

Tadpoles grow
and change into
frogs. Their tails
go away and
they hop on land.

Most frogs need to stay wet. They live near ponds, rivers, or **swamps**.

Some frogs have sticky pads on their toes. These help frogs climb trees and hang on to plants.

Most frogs eat **insects**. They use their tongues to catch insects.

Frogs **croak**, peep, and make other sounds. Frogs can make a lot of noise!

Glossary

croak—to make a deep, rough sound

insects—small animals with six legs and hard outer bodies; insect bodies are divided into three parts.

swamps—land areas that are partly or mostly covered with water for much of the year

tadpoles—young frogs; tadpoles have long tails, breathe with gills, and live in water.

To Learn More

AT THE LIBRARY

Arnosky, Jim. *All About Frogs*. New York, N.Y.: Scholastic, 2002.

Bishop, Nic. *Frogs*. New York, N.Y.: Scholastic, 2008.

Hawes, Judy. *Why Frogs Are Wet*. New York, N.Y.: HarperCollins, 2000.

ON THE WEB

Learning more about frogs is as easy as 1, 2, 3.

1. Go to www.factsurfer.com.

2. Enter "frogs" into the search box.

3. Click the "Surf" button and you will see a list of related Web sites.

With factsurfer.com, finding more information is just a click away.

Index

The images in this book are reproduced through the courtesy of: Ian Wes/Photolibrary, front cover; F. Rauschenbach/Photolibrary, p. 5; Juan Martinez, pp. 7, 19 (left, middle); Kris Holland, p. 7 (left); Steve Bower, p. 7 (right); Steen Drozd Lund/Photolibrary, p. 9; Carl Buchanan/Photolibrary, p. 11; Dr. Morley Read, p. 13; Tim Flach/Getty Images, p. 15; Eduard Kyslynskyy, p. 17; Buddy Mays/Alamy, p. 19; Geanina Bechea, p. 19 (right); Otto Hahn/Photolibrary, p. 21.

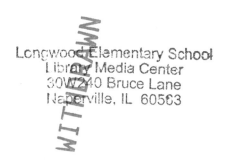